Genealogy, the Internet & You

Good luck
finding stuff on the
'net

Ton

Genealogy, the Internet & You

Andrew M. Pomeroy

ISBN 0-9713804-11-8
Library of Congress Control Number: 2003101468

First Edition   10 9 8 7 6 5 4 3 2

Published by

continuum
202 Viking Avenue
Brea, CA 92821
714-674-0023
www.creativecontinuum.com

Table of Contents

Key Topics

What Does the Internet Offer Me?

Some people might retort, "What doesn't the Internet offer you?" From its inception, the Internet has served one primary purpose – to facilitate the sharing of information. As a genealogist you live to find and share information. The Internet can facilitate your research, your ability to collaborate with others, and your ability to disseminate data. The Internet provides tools and resources to handle a variety of tasks. You are most likely familiar with many of these tools, while others may remain somewhat a mystery but no less worthy of your attention.

Once you better understand and appreciate the tools available you can practice incorporating these tools into your research. In time, you may even develop an itch to share your information by building your own website.

Internet Tools for Genealogist

"Internet" has become the catch-all phrase to describe the worldwide collection of computers, software, tools, and technologies working in tandem to facilitate the sharing of information. Listed below are some of the tools you may find beneficial as a genealogist. Each is briefly described and evaluated for its utility.

The underlying key to understand the Internet is to understand the client/server relationship. When you dine out at a restaurant your waitress is your server and you are the client. Your waitress provides you a service. She takes your order, brings you your food, and keeps your glass full. As the client you won't get any service if you don't first find a service provider. You must go to the restaurant. Once there you may choose anything you want from the menu, but you are limited to the menu. You must also pay for the service you receive.

The Internet operates like a restaurant. Your computer is the client. Many services exist to choose from, like websites. These services reside on and are provided by remote computers called servers. To get service from the server you must first contact the server. Ther server returns information much like a watiress brings food to your table. The client/server relationship is core to the Internet experience.

Following are key services available via the Internet. In all cases, you must use software on you computer specifically designed to work with or access the specific service. Even services like email, where you send messages to a specific person or address, require the use of a server. Email addresses actually represent "mailboxes" which reside on servers. Recipients must access these mailboxes with their own client software to download and read their messages. Read on for more about the specific services available.

Email

Email, or electronic mail, is the digital age's alternative to the written letter. Instead of sending information by stuffing paper into envelopes you can send messages over the Internet. Of course, email is only good for sending information. I don't think anyone has yet found a way to send a box of homemade fudge or that Christmas fruitcake through email, but...

Email is fast and tireless. You can send message around the world in seconds. After all, electronics means using electrons which travel at near light speed across wires or through the atmosphere. Blink and your message is there. With email you can send messages, pictures, data files, and more. Email can seem like the perfect tool to send information to a specific recipient.

Email may also appear as the perfect replacement for the handwritten letter. Not true. Many people feel email is cold and lacks the personal subtlety of traditional mail. Many people don't take the time to think out what they should say in an email. People actually tend to spend more time composing written letters. True, a well-crafted email is every bit as efficient in communicating ideas as any letter. Email has another advantage; people are more likely to respond quickly to email than they are to written letters.

Sending letters, on the other hand, adds a personal touch. People still appreciate the effort you make in writing, folding, and licking [stamps]; something missing from email. Handwritten letters take the personal touch beyond the common. If you take the time to add the personal touch of a handwritten paper letter, then the recipient is likely to spend more time carefully preparing a response.

An email message can be a great way for genealogist to quickly establish possible relationships with others working on the Internet. However, requests for actual information may still be best handled through traditional mail. Deciding which technique to use is usually best determined by getting to know each individual resource. Work at the comfort level of your coconspirator; don't force them to work on your level.

> **Special Note:** *Even better than email or traditional mail is a phone call. Just the sound of your voice may make somebody's day. Voice inflections also transmit meaning often missing from written communications.*

Common use for email:
- Contact individuals
- Conduct geographically distant interviews
- Routinely communicate with others faster and cheaper than via traditional mail

Usenet

News services are among the oldest services on the Internet still available today. Usenet is often described as a worldwide discussion system, a conference system, or an electronic bulletin board. Usenet is a set of "newsgroups" organized hierarchically by topic and name. Some of the highest level groupings include the following:

comp - computing
rec - recreation
misc - miscellaneous
news – commercial news feeds
talk – philosophical, social and political discussions
sci – science

soc – society, culture and genealogy
alt – alternate discussions

Examples of some actual newsgroup names are:

sci.med.dentistry
sci.med.nutrition
sci.space.news
sci.space.shuttle

From the examples you can see the how the newsgroups are organized hierarchically. Sci for science, then medicine or space. Each is then broken down by topic dentistry, nutrition, news, or shuttle. There are over 50,000 newsgroups on the Internet. Possibly many times that number if all languages were counted. Your Internet Service Provider (ISP) determines which newsgroups are available to you.

Each newsgroup is a container for messages, called "articles." Messages are "threaded," meaning original

Sample of Standard news reader software.

messages and all responses are linked. You can easily see where a subject of discussion begins, what responses are made and responses to responses. Usenet works like email, only the messages you send are posted for the world to see and not just sent to select individuals. Some newsgroups are monitored, which means all postings are first read and authorized by a moderator.

Genealogist can find dozens of newsgroups covering topics of history, culture, general genealogy issues, and many dedicated to specific surnames. Newsgroups help put you in contact with other researchers and experts. However, always be cautious. Spend time reading postings to a group before you decide if you want to post a message or question. Be careful of what you say and how you say it. You don't want to jump in with both feet and accidentally offend someone. There is always someone who is easily offended. Make a mistake and you might get "flamed." Flames are message or emails sent to the "offending" party that often ridicule, spite, name

Smith surname board on Ancestry.

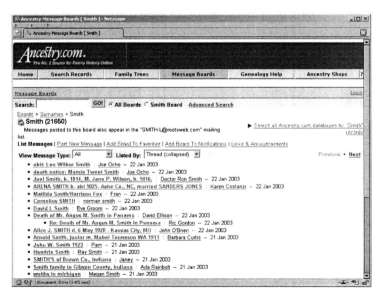

call and worse. Don't be afraid, just be polite and cautious, and never try and sell anything on a newsgroup or you may never hear the end of it.

Message Boards

The improving technology used in developing websites has made the web a solitary challenger to otherwise diverse Internet tools. Message boards are the web equivalent of Usenet and early Bulletin Boards. Web-based message boards operate like Usenet, usually with a hierarchical structure by topic and threaded messaging. Ancestry and Genealogy.com are just a few of the many genealogical sites offering messaging services.

Mailing Lists

Mailing lists are electronic newsletters and discussions transmitted via email. Mailing lists are maintained by software packages that automatically distributes an email message from one subscriber (list member) to all other subscribers on the list. Some lists are moderated, some are for distribution only, while others allow member to create or reply to messages as they choose.

Like Usenet, mailing lists can be a great way to find people who are experts or people passionate in your area of research. Many private organizations now offer limited mailing lists on very specific topics within a field of study. Genealogists are perhaps the luckiest researchers by sheer volumes of mailing lists available. Many major genealogy web sites, including familysearch.org and rootsweb.com offer thousands of mailing lists on specific names and topics.

IRC/Instant Messaging

Internet Relay Chat is the telephone on the Internet. Except, you have to type everything you want to say, and uh… no sound. Every case of Internet infidelity ever touted on the 11 o'clock news began in a chat room. People question IRC: tool or toy? Real addictions have occurred with people spending hours a day locked in chat rooms telling every horrifying detail of their very private lives to total strangers.

IRC is a collection of "channels," usually named by topic, which users may access to converse (type conversations) with other individuals or groups. Topics range from politics to social events to very, very personal information, and more.

Similar in purpose to IRC, instant messaging software allows users with access to the Internet to "talk" with each other. Instead of joining channels on an IRC service, you simply send a message directly to your intended recipient, like email. Assuming the other person is connected to the Internet at the same time, they receive your message and a conversation ensues. Unlike IRC, however, both parties must have the same Instant Messaging software on their respective computers. Instant Messaging is also non-searchable; you must know your intended recipient's call sign or screen name (their address) to establish a connection.

Personally, I feel using IRC and instant messaging are utter wastes of time. Sometimes you might get lucky and stray upon a truly intelligent and enlightened conversation, but don't count on it. IRC is a social tool (toy), not a research tool. The one possible exception is you can arrange to meet someone at a specific time in a private chat room to conduct an interview or hold a focused discussion. I would only suggest IRC as an alternative if a phone call is too expensive or impractical. Neither is a likely scenario.

Things a genealogist might do with IRC:

- Replace a phone call with a chat session
- Setup an impromptu on-line family reunion
- Conduct interviews

FTP

FTP is a protocol, a service, common name for an Internet tool, and an acronym – there is no winning with this one. FTP (File Transfer Protocol) is quite possibly one of the best tools ever developed for sharing data files across a network.

FTP is perhaps the oldest active tool on the Internet today. FTP allows users to directly upload and download files. Files are sent to and from FTP servers using FTP software. Many organizations put files on FTP servers so users and clients can download files at their own leisure.

Web browsers have simplified the FTP process in many ways. Most browsers can access FTP services and download files using only the browser software. However, in most cases third-party software is needed to upload files to FTP servers.

FTP is the most common method of uploading webpages to webserver. The webserver performs the multiple role providing both FTP and Web services. Genealogist deciding to host their own website will likely use FTP to upload their pages.

The FTP benefit to genealogists is simple – think document repository. FTP has served a major role in document repositories for years. Many documents you find and download will likely reside on FTP servers. However, in research you are not likely to upload files.

Your primary concern is to gather data. You will most likely never need any tool more than your web browser to access the files you gather from FTP sources, unless you host your own site.

WWW (World Wide Web)

This is the biggie! The World Wide Web has become synonymous with the Internet. WWW is by far the most poplar and populous tool on the Internet. The web is also one of the youngest tools. The web gained popularity because of its graphical interface and relative ease of use. The web has become both an icon in American culture and a pathway to greater global communications.

You doubt? When was the last time someone asked you, "Are you on-line?" Five or six years ago you may not have understood the question. Guaranteed, today you know the answer. "Yes, I have access." "Yes, I have an email account." "No, I still don't understand how it works, but Andy (that's me) says I don't need to understand how it works to successfully use the Web." How very true. You don't need to understand the intricacies of the combustion engine to productively use an automobile. There are, however, some key points and words of caution you should try to remember:

- You do not need to know how the Internet works, but you do need to understand how to access and use the available tools.
- The World-Wide Web is the largest tool on the Internet today.
- Most of the other tools mentioned are now available through a webpage front end. That means you can access, for example, email from your Internet provider's website.

- Many search tools used to find information on the web also provide non-web information, for example, news postings.
- Most people have come to equate the Web with the Internet. Truly the two are becoming inseparable by distinction, except perhaps among computer geeks like me. However, the Web is still just one element of the Internet.
- Unlike many of the other tools, the Web offers an entirely graphical experience.

Webpages are designed to display content. Content can mean text, graphics, videos, slide shows, results from database queries, and much more. All these media option are available because your web browser is designed to display this information according to guidelines outlined in the actual webpages sent to your computer from websites.

Genealogists clearly gain many benefits from the Web. Like the Internet as a whole, the World-Wide Web has greatly expanded research and collaboration possibilities.

Uses include:

- Finding and sharing family trees
- Finding vital records
- Access to census records
- Posting your own records and family newsletters
- Directory to non-web resources. Using the web like a giant, convenient yellow pages.

Personal Websites

Personal websites have become a huge trend among genealogists. Most Internet Service Providers (ISPs) provide website space on their servers for their customers. Many third-party services also make websites available to individuals for a small fee or sometimes even for free. Genealogists by the hundreds use these small free and inexpensive websites to post their genealogy. It can be very exciting to tell your family all they need to do is look the information up on your site.

Most of today's competitive genealogy software includes the ability to export family databases into web-ready (HTML) format. Most applications create surname indexes and plain-text links. Web-based pedigrees and family information in this basic formatting rarely look very pretty. However, the ability to access ancestral information from anywhere in the world is an exciting prospect. Both collaboration among distant relatives and finding information for your own research becomes easier as more sites become available.

Choose a favorite search engine and type in the surname you are looking for. Assuming the name you type is not a famous person or common object, then most of the search results will likely point to these types of personal websites.

> **Special Note:** *Please beware. If you are planning on creating your own family site be warned - do not invade your family's right to privacy.*

I have seen websites with the names, birthdates and other vital information clearly given for living children and adults. On the same site I can often find the submitter's address and phone number. One look at such a list and I could know where the person lives, how many children likely live at home, what their ages are, and their gender. Personally, I have no need for such information. Unfortunately, there are many people in this world who would choose to exploit such knowledge for personal gain and satisfaction. You don't even want to think about what such a person might do. Think ahead and protect yourself.

Software is available, sometimes built into your family history software, which lets you remove "living" information when you create a website. Use these tools. You probably don't want your children's names even mentioned and never include birthdates.

Posting family pedigrees is alluring to genealogists. The practice makes practical sense to researchers. If you feel inclined to create your own website, don't hesitate, make the effort.

Regardless if you post your own pedigrees or research the sites of others, be mindful of privacy concerns. Protect yourself and your children by planning ahead.

.

2 Working on the Web

Knowing Your Browser Better

There are only three operating systems likely to be found on a home computer; Windows®, Mac OS® (for Apple systems), or Linux. Most home system run Windows. Apple Macs take a distant second with Linux in last place but coming on strong. Both the Mac and Windows systems support the World's two most popular web browsers, Netscape and Internet Explorer. Linux supports Mozilla–a Netscape derivative. This section covers some simple tips and guides to help you get the most out of your web browser.

"Best viewed with Internet Explorer." This is just the type of claim you have undoubtedly come across on occasion. Many sites claim you need to use Netscape over IE, and vice versa. Web developers make this claim due to slight variances between the two applications. Both programs can open virtually any site on the web. However, some key technologies, like scripting support, may act differently one brand to the next. The nuances are typically minor and should not be a point of discouragement for the average user. Choosing between browsers is like choosing between a white Honda Accord and a white Toyota Corolla. Both cars are priced about the same, both get good gas mileage, look similar, handle well, have about the same amount of power and similar safety records. So which one do you pick? The answer is one of personal preference. Some people go for the name, some past experience, others on what they believe to be an educated selection. In the end, most people are satisfied with their choice. The same holds true for web browsers. Personal choice and preferences have led to a lot of bickering over the years between the Netscape and Internet Explorer factions, but in the end both perform equally well.

Internet Explorer at FamilySearch website

Compare to Netscape: both look very similar.

In each, the webpage is displayed equally well. Only the application window (the frame) looks a little different.

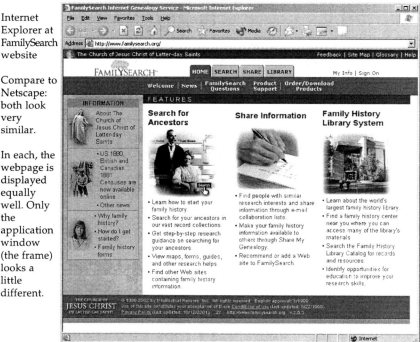

"So Andy, which do you use?" Easy, both. As a professional web developer I make the effort to ensure all my design works equally well in both applications. I concern myself with the nuances between browsers so my clients don't have to. As we discuss browsers in greater detail I will use example from both browsers. You will find that changing the way a button looks does little to change the way it acts, and in that alone lies the greatest difference between these two popular browsers.

Netscape at FamilySearch website

Compare to Internet Explorer: both look very similar.

Before going on, I will acknowledge there are other browsers out there. Most will support the same features and work in much the same manner as the two discussed here. This review is focused on enhancing the users search and browsing skills and learning to make better use of the available tools regardless of brand.

Your Interface to the Web

The browser is an independent application. You can open a web browser without actually connecting to the Internet. The window, the primary shell of the web browser is called the Interface. Take a look at some of the key elements of the Interface:

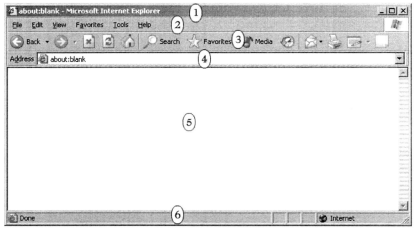

1 Title Bar
2 Menu Bar
3 Button Bar
4 Address Bar
5 Document Window
6 Status Bar

Title Bar

The title bar displays both the title for the webpage currently showing as well as the name of the browser you are using.

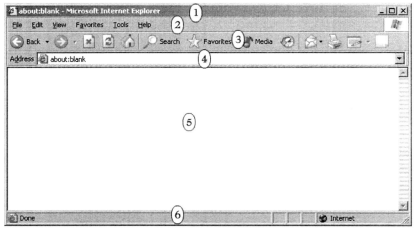

Example:

> "FamilySearch Internet Genealogy Service" is the name of the website/webpage and "Netscape" is the name of the browser.

Menu Bar

The menu bar gives you access to all the standard functions you would expect from any application, as well as those specific to the web browser. Features like save, print, copy, options and preferences are all available from the menu bar.

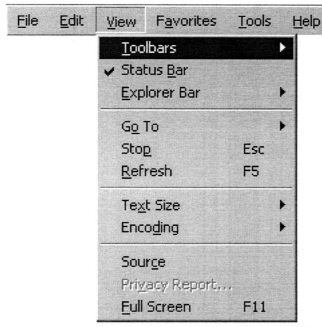

Menu bar
from
Internet
Explorer

The names for menus items and the specific functions may vary somewhat between brands but the functionality is consistent.

Most browsers allow you to bookmark pages (sometimes called favorites). You can change default settings or view the source code for a webpage. These features become increasingly advantageous as your experience on the Web grows.

Don't be afraid to click on menu items you don't recognize. Hands-on experience is always the best way to learn.

Button and Address Bars

Buttons are nothing more than graphical links to functions otherwise found on the menu bar. The buttons on your web browser's button bar are designed to help you more quickly navigate the Web. Here are both Internet Explorer's and Netscape's button bars:

Internet Explorer uses a distinct button bar and a separate address bar (shown above). Netscape takes a different approach. Netscape uses a navigation bar, mixing navigation buttons and the address element on one bar. A second bar offers buttons for additional features (below).

Again, the functionality is consistent across both browsers even if the actual position and look of the individual buttons and bars are different.

In the following section, website address are examined in greater detail. The Address bar shows the user what page or site he is currently browsing. The bar also allows the user to type in an address and quickly transfer to the desired page. If you already know you want to go directly to genealogy.com it is usually faster to type geanealogy.com into the address bar than it is to find the link within your favorites (bookmark) list.

There are many buttons on the button bar. The most useful are the navigation buttons. Each is described below showing both the Internet Explorer (IE) and Netscape (NS) equivalents:

Back

Returns the user to the previously viewed webpage. Includes a drop-down list (use the small down arrow) of the past 10 or so pages viewed. The drop-down list allow you to quickly return to a page multiple links back. IE NS

Forward

As the name implies, it is opposite of the back button. Once the back feature has been used, the forward button is used to return the user to his starting point. The user can only move as far forward as the page he was at before moving backwards. In some cases the forward feature also provides a drop down list to allow users to move multiple pages forward at one time. IE NS

Stop

Sometimes a page is stuck, not fully loaded. Other times the user clicks the wrong link and doesn't want to wait for the next page to load before going back. The stop button stops the download of a webpage. If a partial page is loaded a IE NS simple click of the back button returns the user to the previous page.

Refresh

Also called the reload button. Click this button and the browser sends a message to the web server saying, "send me a fresh copy of the webpage." The refreshed page is displayed.

The refresh is commonly used for two key reasons. Sometime a page will not successfully load and an error is returned. Clicking the reload button is the fastest way to try accessing the page again. Many webpages are dynamic by nature. These pages display updated content on a regular basis. To make sure the latest information is currently displayed, hit the refresh page and the most current data flows down from the server.

Home

Every web browser allow the user to choose a "home" page. The home page is the webpage that is automatically displayed when the browser is opened. The home button will quickly return the user to the browser's default page at anytime the user is online.

Favorites

Internet Explorer uses the term favorites, Netscape uses bookmarks. Both browser allow the user to keep a list of interesting website. When the user clicks this button the favorites list is displayed. Each item on the list is a link to a webpage.

A user can add an item to their favorites/bookmarks by simply holding down the Ctrl and D keys together (Windows option).

Whatís in an Address

Look at the address in the figure below:

> 🔍 http://boards.ancestry.com/mbexec/board/an/surnames.smith| ▼

The address for the website is *boards.ancestry.com.* Do you know what the address really means? Knowing the parts of the address may help you better navigate both the web and the Internet. The address is actually broken into parts. A URL (Uniform Resource Locator) is the entire context of the address line, from the http to the last character. The actual web address is only the first part between the double forward slash, "//," and the first single slash, "/." For example, www.familysearch.org is an entire web address.

Web addresses are common names used to represent the numerical IP address. The technology used on the Internet translates the common address you type on your web browser into an IP address. One IP address for Microsoft is 207.46.134.222. Which address are you going to remember, microsoft.com or 207.46.134.222? Most people will remember the common name address.

The Internet is organized hierarchically so that names are translated to numerical addresses as quickly as possible. The name is actually evaluated in reverse order. The final element .com, .org, etc. represents the highest level in the naming hierarchy. To enhance our discussion we will break the address into its key elements and look at it in reverse order.

Domain

The .com, .org., .net and similar extensions are at the highest level. These are called domains. Each represents a class or hierarchy in the naming conventions of the Internet. Until recently there were only six major domains dedicated to specific uses:

Domain	Purpose
.com	commercial
.org	non profit organizations
.net	network/Internet providers
.edu	education
.gov	government
.mil	military

In actuality, any person, group, or company could obtain .com, .org, or .net addresses at will. The other three addresses were limited to their appropriate group. In other words, you had to be a certified educational facility to obtain an .edu domain address, and so forth.

Additional top level domains have more recently been added to the list, including .biz, .name, .info and more.

To complicate matters further, many addresses use country code extensions. The country code is often needed when searching for sites outside the United States, but not mandated. You don't actually need to concern yourself about adding the country code or not. If you are given or find an address to a website and the address includes the country code then use it. If the address is given without the country code, even if you know the server is in another country, then you don't use it.

Genealogist may enjoy knowing what the extensions are for conducting foreign research. It is nice to know what country a website is in when looking for foreign ancestors.

Domain Name

The middle of the address, between the two "." (dots) is the domain name. Ancestry, familysearch, genealogy, to name a few, are well-know domain names to genealogists. Add the ".com" and you are on your way.

The domain name is the site name, the name people remember. Companies have gone to court over these names. If you are Disney you definitely want the Disney.com name.

Sometimes multiple names get pointed to the same website. F a m i l y s e a r c h . c o m , familysearch.org, and familysearch.net all point to the same website.

Genealogy.com and genealogy.net do not point to the same site. The name or names you own as an individual, company or group depend on which ones you choose to buy and register.

www

Here the address gets a little more complex. First of all, not all sites use www.

The address element, commonly "www," placed just before the domain name represents a specific location within a domain. Www is the default name on most web servers. However a company may choose to change the name to something other than www. In addition, a company's network may be setup to allow any web requests to access the default server without specifically identifying the server by name. Larger organizations simply have too many services to run under a single name or on a single computer. Using alternative identifiers in a web address let companies point each request from the client's browser to the exact location within a domain.

http://

These first few characters represent the protocol used on the Web. HTTP stands for Hyper-Text Transfer Protocol. This is the technology that lets you click a link and get bounced to the next webpage. This part of the address simply tells your browser the type of communication you want to have over the Internet. "Http://," says, "I want a webpage."

Special Note: most browsers allow you to type an address without typing 'http://.' The web browser assumes this protocol by default.

Take another look at our first example:

> http://boards.ancestry.com/mbexec/board/an/surnames.smith

Http://boards.ancestry.com. You now have what is called a Fully-Qualified Domain Name (FQDN). Look again at the complete address, what is all the information after the FQDN?

In the sample address, everything after the first single forward slash represents directories and files located on the web server. Everything after the domain name points to a file on the server and may contain information to be processed by the file. The entire address from beginning to end, as mentioned above, is called the URL.

I don't want to confuse you with too many details and possible variations, so I will leave the topic here. Just remember, the first part is the FQDN – the website address. Everything after the single slash is a pointer to specific information provided by the service.

Searching Within

Hopefully, you are well acquainted with search engines. Engines like AltaVista and Google provide links to websites based on keyword queries. Type in genealogy and get a list of sites and pages using the keyword genealogy. Research using search engines is a skill of its own (see my book *Mastering Search Engines*). However, finding a site is only half the battle.

Often when you use a search engine or a directory like Cyndi's List you are linked to the main or home page of a website. What you need is the page with the specific information you are looking for. Other times you link to the page you need but there is so much information presented you cannot find the part you need. I have been to sites where entire books, hundreds of pages of text, are placed on a single webpage. Thousands of words, hundred of paragraphs and all I want is the tidbit on my great grand-whomever. Many applications, including most web browsers have a tool to help. The find tool.

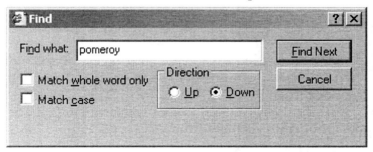

Find will locate a text string within the body of a webpage. In most cases the find tool is accessible in a couple of ways. You can use your mouse or keyboard, go to the menu bar, select edit, and select find. In Windows, you can hold the control key down and hit the "F" key, Ctrl+F. The find dialog box opens.

Type the word or string you are looking for and click the "Enter" key or mouse-click the "Find" button. The page moves to the first instance of your string on the page and highlights the word(s). Click find again to move to the next instance.

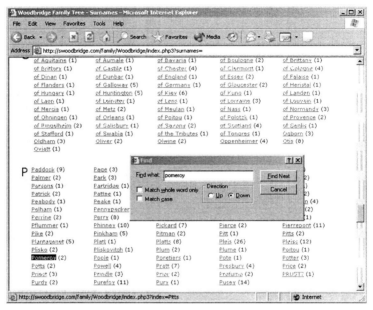

Sometimes even relatively short pages are so cluttered you need the find tool to see the words already in front of you.

The best part of the find tool is its availability. The tool is built into virtually any software package you use. Try using find in your email software or your word processing package. You will be delighted in how much easier it is to find and access information in large documents.

3 Did You Know

Sometimes we work with tools or technologies to the point we become experts in their use yet we know little of their history or actual functionality. I am sure most of you are expert drivers. But, could you look under the hood and decribe the various parts of the engine and how they work? Could you open up your computer, identify and replace components?

You might not need to know how a clock ticks to keep time, however, knowlege does increase confidence and provides reassurance. The more you know about how your car functions the more confident you are the mechanic is not trying to rip you off.

Sometimes, it is just fun to learn more about the tools you use. This section is to provide added knowledge about the tools you use as a genealogist. This section is meant to both entertain and educate.

Soundex

With the introduction of Social Security in 1935 the new social program needed a method to qualify the age of applicants who could not provide documentation of their birth. The government created a department called the "Age Search Group" to fix the problem. The group began searching census records, but realized the enormity of the task was impossible without some kind of index. The Census Bureau hired the Rand Corporation to develop a workable index. Thus was born Soundex.

The Soundex system works by sound not by spelling. Names in census records were often misspelled or families changed the spelling as time passed. Using a sound based index, spelling becomes less relevant than the sound of a name. Someone searching the index doesn't need to guess at alternative spellings, all options are returned in a search.

The Age Search Group began by indexing the 1880 census for households with children under the age of 10. This established a list of individuals who were of qualifying age in 1935. The Census Bureau hired clerks from the Works Progress Administration (WPA) to index the census using the new Soundex system. After the 1880 census was completed the 1900 and 1920 censuses were also indexed. The 1910 census wasn't indexed until the 1960s and was the first census compiled by computer.

The Soundex index cards created in the process include the name, age, and birthplace for head-of-household, and all those living in the household with their relationship to the head-of-house. The Soundex is used to find the state, county, E.D. number and page number for family information in the census schedules. The entire census record can then be accessed.

How exactly does the Soundex work

As mentioned above, surnames are often distorted or changed over time. Illiteracy, poorly written or damaged records, misunderstandings, and human error have all led to inaccuracies in the censuses and indexes. Soundex was designed to minimize the difficulties resulting from such errors.

Soundex is a method to encode surnames such that all similar names are found during a search. Names like Freiley, Frailey and Fraily all have the same Soundex code. Search any one of these names and all are returned. I know a Freiley doing her family history. She found many ancestors she might not have found if not for the Soundex. The census records she researched contained different spellings of her name.

How is a Soundex code generated?

The Soundex rules are actually quite easy.

1. All Soundex codes are four digits long.
2. The first digit is a letter, followed by three numbers. For example, all three names above (Freiley, Frailey, and Fraly) encode as F640. The author's last name, Pomeroy, encodes as P560
3. Encode names using these guidelines:

The letter of the code is always the first letter of the last name.
     Pomeroy = P

Example:
Building the code for Pomeroy

P_ _ _

The numbers are filled in from the following chart, working with the name left to right for each remaining letter of the name:

Numerical Code	For these Letters
1	B, F, P, V
2	C, G, J, K, Q, S, X, Z
3	D, T
4	L
5	M, N
6	R

A, E, I, O, U, H, W, and Y have no numerical representation.

P56 _   P̶o̶m̶e̶r̶o̶y̶ : m = 5; r = 6

If not enough characters exist to fill in all three numbers then zeros ("0") are used to fill in unused spaces.

P560   P̶o̶m̶e̶r̶o̶y̶ = 0 left; use 0

These additional rules apply:

Double letters are treated as one letter.
Kelly is coded K400

Consecutive, non-duplicate consonants with equivalent numerical values are treated as one letter.

Pfeifer = P160 (P, skip F, 1 for F, 6 for R, 0 to fill)

Hickman = H250 (H, 2 for C, skip K, skip M, 5 for N, 0 to fill) M not coded, see below

Surname prefixes like Von, Van, Con, De, Li, etc. (usually meaning "from" or "of") are ignored as a rule. Some systems may include the name twice;

with and without the prefix. Note that Mac, Mc, and O' are not prefixes, these are part of the proper name.

> DiCapprio = C160 (C, 1 for P, skip P, 6 for R, 0 to fill)
>
> McNair = M256 (M, 2 for C, 5 for N, 6 for R)

If a vowel (A, E, I, O, U) separates two consonants that have the same Soundex code, the consonant to the right of the vowel is coded

> Hickman = H250 (H, 2 for C, skip K, skip M, 5 for N, 0 to fill) M is not coded because M and N are separated by the vowel A.

If "H" or "W" separate two consonants that have the same Soundex code, the consonant to the right of the vowel is **not** coded.

> Ashcraft = A-261 (A, 2 for the S, skip C, 6 for R, 1 for F).

What is the Soundex code for your surname:

_____

Soundex has proven a wonderful tool for searching census records. However, Soundex was designed for and works best with names written using English phonetics. The closer a name is written to match its English pronunciation the better the Soundex coding works. The more foreign and unusual a name is the more likely complications and errors will occur when applying Soundex.

GEDCOM

If you have spent even one day in researching your family history you have probably heard this term. But, do you know what it means?

GEDCOM is an acronym, short for **GE**nealogical **D**ata **COM**munication. The Church of Jesus Christ of Latter-day Saints developed the flexible and uniform format for exchanging genealogical data. The GEDCOM standard (set of rules for creating a GEDCOM file) allows users with different programs to share their family databases. Virtually all genealogy programs can create a GEDCOM file of your information. You can then share the file with others. You can save the file to a diskette and mail it or you can send the file attached to an email message. You can even upload your GEDCOM file to Family Search or similar sites via the Internet.

GEDCOM Today

A GEDCOM file is actually a simple method to structure information and maintain relationships between individuals. If you open a GEDCOM file with a text reader/editor like Notepad (in Windows) the information would look something like this:

```
0 INDI
  1 NAME John Smith
  1 BIRT
    2 DATE 14 JAN 2002
    2 PLAC Fullerton, Orange, California, USA
0 INDI
  1 NAME Jane Smith
  1 BIRT
    2 DATE 14 DEC 2002
    2 PLAC Fullerton, Orange, California, USA
```

Other information would be listed for each individual as would be found in the database. Where information in your pedigree is blank (e.g. a missing date) then those lines are simply omitted from the GEDCOM file. This streamlines the file, making it smaller and more manageable. Additional information under each individual would also connect the person to parents and to marriages. Marriage records are listed in the same method starting with "0 MARR."

& *Tomorrow*

The GEDCOM standard has worked for many years and has helped thousands share their family data. The current GEDCOM standard version is 5.5. The next generation, version 6.0, is in Beta (testing) format. The new standard is a major change from the past. To better adapt to new and merging technologies, including the Internet, the new standard is built upon the XML language model. XML stands for eXtensible Markup Language. The new format replaces marker information (e.g. "0 INDI") with markup tags (e.g. "<Individual>"). Markup tags come both before and after each value to clearly identify pertinent data. Compare the previous example with this XML example for the individual record of John Smith:

```
<IndividualRec Id="IN01">
  <IndivName>
    <NamePart Type="given name" Level="2">John
    </NamePart>
    <NamePart Type="surname" Level="1">Smith
    </NamePart>
  </IndivName>

</IndividualRec>
```

```
<EventRec Id="EV01" Type="birth" VitalType="birth">
  <Participant>
    <Link Target="IndividualRec" Ref="IN01"/>
  </Participant>
  <Date>14 JAN 2002</Date>
  <Place>
    <PlacePart Type="town" Level="4">Fullerton
    </PlacePart>
    <PlacePart Type="county" Level="3">Orange
    </PlacePart>
    <PlacePart Type="state" Level="2">California
    </PlacePart>
    <PlacePart Type="country" Level="1">USA
    </PlacePart>
  </Place>
</EventRec>
```

The good news is you will never be expected to manually create this record. You never had to in the past and you won't need to in the future. What is important to understand is the new format will add additional flexibility and capabilities to your software and your ability to collaborate with others.

A complete white paper on the GEDCOM XML version 6.0 Beta standard is available on the included CD.

Pictures Make it Pretty

"I have been looking everywhere for a picture of my Grandmother. I finally found one on my cousin's website. I printed the picture on my super deluxe photo inkjet printer on expensive, glossy photo paper and it looked awful! I took the file to the copy center and printed it on the color laser printer, really expensive, and it looks bad, too. Why won't my print come out? The image on my cousin's site looks real clear, real good. What's wrong with my printer or with my system?"

I have heard statements like these countless times. The answer is simple. Nothing is wrong with your printer or your computer or even the picture on the website. The problem is the image resolution of Grandma's picture is set for screen viewing only, too low for print quality. To explain this clearly there are two important aspects of images and image quality you must understand. First is the difference between continuous tone and bitmapped images. The second is resolution, defined in dots-per-inch.

When you take a picture with a traditional camera you use optics (lens) to reflect a near perfect impression of your subject onto light-sensitive film. The image is captured exactly as it appears in real life. Film is chemically altered to create the negative. Light is again passed through lenses and the negative to reflect the image onto light-sensitive paper. A chemical bath for the paper and voilà, a photograph.

A photograph is an uninterrupted or continuous image. The image is an exact replication of the original.

Images captured with digital cameras or photographs scanned onto a computer are altered from their original state. Computers are incapable of saving images in continuous tone. Images are captured by digitizing the source. Both scanners and digital cameras use CCDs (Charge Coupled Devices) to capture images as a series of dots, called pixels. The more dots per inch (a.k.a. dpi) an image has the greater the image quality. Higher resolution equals greater quality.

No matter how close together the dots get, the image is still represented as dot and not a continuous tone. As technology improves, the dots will get smaller and closer together. Eventually these dots will get so small that the human eye won't be able to tell the difference between a high quality digital image and a continuous tone photograph.

Pictures on the Web

Monitors, the TV-looking part of you computer system, typically display 72 or 96 dots per inch – 72dpi or 96dpi. Regardless whether an image is saved with a low dpi or a high dpi, on screen the image will generally look good. Both a high-resolution image file and low-resolution image file display at 96dpi. Both images look the same. This visual equality does not hold true when high and low resolution images are printed.

Low resolution images comparitively do not look as good as high-resolution files when printed. The minimum resolution for print quality images is 300dpi. Anything less than 300 and the dots are too far apart to fool the eye. The dots pattern is too noticeable. The result is rough edges and distorted colors. The effect is called pixilation.

Contrary to popular myth, forcing the computer to print a low-resolution image at a higher dpi does not make the lower quality image look better. Trying to manipulate the settings only forces the computer to compensate by adding extra dots. To create the extra dots the computer interpolates the image, it makes a guess. Interpolation creates additional dots based on the color in surrounding dots. The resulting image looks no better than the original 72dpi print. The edges may be smoother but color is distorted and the image appears blurry.

The image from our first example of grandma printed from cousin Bill's website looked great on screen but not in print. Grandma's image was saved as a 72dpi file.

Look at these two examples:

72 dpi image

File Size:
74.4 KB color
33.7 KB black & white

300 dpi image

File Size:
1.98 MB (1,980 KB) color
470 KB black & white

Special Note: *Both these images look identical on screen. Printed the images look signicifantly different.*

Are you wondering why cousin Bill doesn't just save higher-resolution images on his website so you can download and print with high clarity? The answer is two part. First, not all cameras and scanners are made equal. The more affordable the camera or scanner the lower the dpi image it will produce. The higher the dpi the higher the cost. Second, the higher the dpi of an image the larger the computer file size will be. The relationship is exponential. A small resolution gain registers a large increase in needed hard drive space and longer transfer/download time.

Consider the ramifications of larger files sizes on the Internet. The larger the file the longer it takes to download and display. Plus, remember many personal sites are free but small. It does not take long to fill up free web space when uploading large files into a webpage.

Genealogists should consider the ramifications of the images they post to their own sites and those they find in research. The best solution is to show low-resolution copies on the Internet and provide the means in which high-resolution copies can be sent via traditional mail.

Libraries

Where would Genealogy be without the library? Libraries are the Fort Knox of books. A true researcher likely considers the contents of one small library greater in value than all the gold bullion in the World.

The Worldwide Misconception

Never before has humankind been able to share information at the speeds made possible by the Internet. The Worldwide Web offers unparalleled access to vast resources available from around the globe. The technology and worldwide adoption of the Web and Internet is a marvel to many. The Web is seen by many as the ultimate repository of information. It's easy to stand in awe of the Web. Such awe at its size and misconceptions about the technologies that make the Net possible have led to the perpetuation of one great myth:

You can find "everything" on the Web.

The truth is, only the smallest fraction of human art and knowledge is available on the Web. Fortunately, the Internet is still growing.

The Good News

Libraries collectively represent a vast collection of human knowledge, far greater than what is available on the Web today. Libraries are also quickly making their resources available over the Internet. Many library catalogs have been available via telnet for many years. However, telnet sessions are difficult for many non-practiced users. More recently many libraries have begun offering web-based services, including the following:
- On-line catalogs
- Full-text magazines and articles
- Biographical profiles
- Full-text books

The Not-Quite-As-Good News

The prospects for on-line library services are exciting. Unfortunately, libraries operate independently of each other. Independent decision making and budget restriction limit some libraries from offering many add-on services. Full-text databases, among other services, require libraries pay third-party suppliers for the data offered library clientele. To control costs, many libraries can only offer these services to their registered patrons. You may need to hold a library card to the specific library in order to gain access to some services.

4 *Security*

You would never walk down the street with your wallet or purse wide open and money sticking out. You would never knowingly ingest poison. You would also probably never intentionally spend time in a closed room with someone carrying a highly-contagious and fatal disease. Why put yourself in harms way? After all, 90% of security is about protecting yourself from harm by avoiding obvious dangers. Yet, everyday people subject themselves and their computers to just these types of pitfalls.

Adults know to hide their money from public view, to avoid people coughing in public, to not take food from strangers, to simply not put their hands into the fire lest they be burnt. Adults learn these rules in childhood. Children gain an education from experience and instruction. To a child such knowledge and such cautious protection may seem overwhelming and difficult. Do you feel any less overwhelmed by the Internet?

Have you ever opened an email attachment and gotten a virus? Have you ever purchased anything online without knowing if the site was secure or not? Most people who use the Internet have done just these things. Worse, there is always the potential of hidden attacks by hackers, con artists, and other "cyber" deviants to monitor your Internet travels or to directly access your machine and steal vital personal information.

Online security, like in the real world, is 90% education. Follow some simple guideline and avoid the pitfalls. Learn the rules of engagement and you increase your chance of survival. Remember, predators usually seek the weakest member of a group. Below are some guidelines to help you survive your Internet childhood.

First Four Steps

1. Download patches and service pack for your operating system and software. As problems with software are found and new security risks discovered software companies issue updates to fix these flaws. The updates are usually called patches and are easily obtained from manufacturer's websites. Sometimes a manufacturer will group a number of patches together into a single installation called a service pack. One of the best defense mechanisms for users is to keep a regular watch for new patches and install these updates as soon as they are released.

   Microsoft has a website dedicated just to operating system patches, located at windowsupdate.microsoft.com.

2. Don't talk to strangers. The most basic common sense rule there is. If you use AOL or Microsoft's instant messaging packages then be absolutely sure you don't talk with strangers. These tools are de-

signed to let you send messages and files back and forth between "peers." They are a type of "peer to peer" networking. However, these applications may expose your IP address (your numeric address on the Internet) to others. With your address in hand a hacker may attempt to access your system. Also, never download files from anyone you do not know and trust.

3. Double check your browser's configuration. Is the security set for your protection? There are numerous security settings that allow or disable options such as reading cookies, pasting information from your clipboard, executing script commands, or even downloading and opening programs. Configure your software for your own protection.

Special Note: If you have Internet Explorer go to browsercheck.qualys.com and test your settings for weaknesses.

4. Download the latest update for your virus protection software. If you don't have virus protection software then go right now and buy a package and install it. New viruses are found all the time. Many viruses are a slightly modified version of older viruses; easy to make but different enough that older software won't recognize the threat. If you don't keep your virus definition files up to date you risk catching a nasty disease.

Password Rules

1. Use complex passwords. The easiest passwords to break are words found in the dictionary and dates. Never use a birthday or anniversary as your

password or pin number. The longer the password the better. Many systems allow you to use upper and lowercase letters, numbers, and special characters (i.e. @,#,$,*,|, etc.). By mixing case and adding non-letter characters you make it much harder for hackers to guess or use password cracking tools to determine your passwords.

2. Use different password for each account. If someone does get one of your passwords your exposure is limited.

3. Never save your passwords on your computer. If your system is hacked the intruder could get enough information to completely take over your identity.

Some Common Sense

1. Never open attachments in email unless you know the sender and know for a fact the file was intentionally sent to you. Many viruses infect one computer then replicate by sending themselves via email to all the users in a person's email address book. You may receive a virus without the sender even knowing it was sent. So unless you know, don't open that attachment.

2. Watch for name extensions when downloading files. A common trick for hiding viruses is to make a file look like an image, media, or text file. In actuality the file may be an executable program. Unless you are intentionally downloading a program then you should not see these extensions at the end of the file name .bat, .vbs, .js, .exe, or .com.

File extensions are often hidden on the PC. If you don't see the full file name including the extension then use the icon to identify what the file type is. Here are some examples of typically safe files icons vs. potentially bad file icons:

 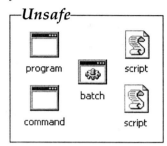

Note, many icons look the same or similar. Often the only difference between one icon type and another is color. For example, the first image icon above is red on screen while the second is green.

3. Don't provide personal information and/or credit card numbers unless you know for sure the business is legitimate.

4. Don't give out your credit card number and information unless the website is secure. The easiest way to check for this is to look at the web address. Does the address begin with https:// instead of the standard http://? The "s" indicates secure or encrypted. Cyber thieves often monitor retail sites and try to steal credit information. Don't enter personal information on large retailer's websites unless you know the site is secure. Smaller retailers present less of a problem. Smaller sites are less likely to be watched. There is some effort involved in recording and monitoring site traffic to pull personal information. The "bad guys" are not likely to waste time with lower traffic retailers.

5. Security on the web is a numbers game. The larger the population the less likely you are to get hurt. If you are comfortable with purchasing from small retailers you trust then you are probably safe.

6. Never make purchases from any site you cannot readily identify as a viable business. Learn to evaluate websites and businesses. Make a phone call before you buy the first time, just to make sure everything is on the up and up.

7. Understand your network. Learn the basics about the type of Internet connection you have (i.e. DSL, Cable, dial-up). Find out if you have a static or dynamic IP address – your ISP can answer that question for you. Dynamic IPs are typically better for home users. When you IP changes so does your ID.

8. Turn off all unneeded services*. This is especially important for Windows NT, 2000, and XP users.

9. Turn off file and print sharing.

Special Note: Find yourself a qualified support technician. Pay for an hour or two worth of service. Have your machine configured and needed software and patches installed.

You'll probably never see an unsuccessful hack attempt or an attempt to steal your identity. It is better to not know if someone tried to ruin your life than to find out the hard way that someone succeeded.

Firewalls

So what is a firewall? Well one definition I found sums it up fairly well, "a device to keep the bad guys out." Not enough? Try this, "A firewall is a network gateway that enforces security rules on the conversion of peer-to-peer communications... A firewall provides a single point of defense between two networks—it protects one network from the other." Let me try. A firewall is a software program or hardware device (both exist) meant to restrict access to your computer or network from the outside world while letting the information through you want to send and receive.

Both software and hardware firewall work to protect your computer but in slightly different ways. Software firewalls are programs you install on your computer that monitor traffic to and from a network (i.e. Internet) and look for packets that break the rules.

Packets are how modern networks transfer data. Think of a packet as an envelope where you can only send part of your letter at a time. You break your letter up and put a piece in many envelopes. Each envelope is sent separately. Networks break your data up into manageable size packets which are sent to the recipient. If a piece of information is missing then a copy of the missing piece is requested from the recipient and retransmitted from the sender. This method reduces error in your data.

Hardware firewalls watch the flow of packets and identify ones that don't belong or break some rule. For example, data sent from an unknown IP address or a request to send data from unknown software on your own system (e.g. a virus sending out information).

The good news is both types of firewalls are fairly inexpensive. The bad new is neither is easily configured. Unless you have a good background in networks and the Internet then either will likely cost you more grief than you feel its worth.

Software firewalls are easier to configure, but can be a constant annoyance, especially at first before all the rules have been established. Often the alerts that pop up are confusing and unclear. Hardware firewalls are typically far more difficult to configure, but you configure once and then let it run. Software firewalls also need installed and configured on every PC while hardware firewalls work well to protect multiple PCs.

The decision can be tough, until you have been hacked and your data laid waste or your identity stolen. Get a firewall and learn how to use it. One day your childhood will pass and you will one day become an Internet adult, but first an education.

5 *Your CD*

As I considered the project that has become this book and CD, I looked for a way to provide something more than the traditional printed "yellow pages" of websites. I sought to provide both a practical means of linking to useful websites, as well as providing additional features impossible to include in printed format. I also wanted the ability to grow the project over time. The result was the handbook and CD combination you now hold.

The book provides a great introduction to key concepts and skills to enhance the Internet Genealogist's experience. The CD allows me to provide manageable content in a updateable and manageable format.

One of the Web's greatest advantages is also its greatest liability, flexibility. For the web developer the ability is create, change, modify and update sites quickly and easily is a wonder unto itself. Such flexibility also makes it difficult to catalog or index the Web. Web pages are changed, deleted, and moved daily. This creates dead links. Dead links are those annoying links you click but lead you nowhere. Worse, your browser often returns an error. You find yourself wondering what happened to Cousin Bill and his website. Large search engine companies like Google and Altavista spend millions of dollars on high-speed computers that do nothing but try and re-index the web every few days just to stay current.

The good news is most top sites change little. At the very least, most homepages are accessible from the same address even when subsequent pages change. Many genealogy sites have changed content and structure over the years but are still available at the same address. The CD takes into consideration possible changes and tries to provide useful tools, links, and articles pertinent to today, enduring over the short run, and modifiable over the long haul.

Accessing the CD

1 Pop the disk into your CD-ROM drive.
2 Off you go.

The CD is designed to run automatically when you put the disk in your computer. If the program does not automatically open, then do the following:

Windows machines:
1 Click Start Button
2 Click Run
3 Type "D:\default.htm" (no quotes; use D or appropriate drive letter for you CD-ROM)

On the Disk

The CD is broken into six major categories. Each category may contain sub categories. All categories mearly serve as structure to provide you ease of use.

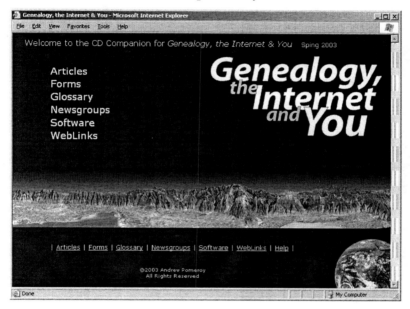

Article & more

A growing list of articles, guides, and documents. Article cover gereral interest, technological, and genealogical interest items. Some of the articles available include:

- A brief history of the Internet
- Set of Genealogical Standards as recommended by the National Genealogical Society
- Country code list for domain names

Specail Note: *all the documents in this section are in PDF format. Adobe's Acrobat Reader is needed to read and*

> *print files. Acrobat Reader is available in the software
> section on the CD in both Windows and Mac versions.*

Forms

Good old-fashioned, fill-in-the-blank forms. A series of research logs and trackers to help organize your family history research. Forms are in PDF format (see special note above). Print these forms and keep them with your research. Good habits breed success.

Sample Form - Research Log:

Glossary

New and relevant terms. Internet and technology terms with simple definittons for those that hate acronyms. Watch out, some of these definitions may throw you for aloop.

Newsgroups

Over 120 news groups of topical interest to gene-alogists. From surname specific to specific cultures, it's about finding what interest you.

Software

What better way to assist the on-line genealogist than to provide useful tools and applications.

Freeware

Software available at no cost to the user. Usu-ally, freeware is provided by a major vendor as a viewer or support application to a full-priced re-tail package. Acrobat Reader is a good example of freeware. The reader allows the user to read PDF files created from Acrobat–a standard re-tail package. Sometimes freeware is simply de-veloped by a hobbyists or program for their own reasons, to the benefit of all.

Shareware/Trialware

Try before you buy software. Shareware appli-cations are available to install and use by the general public, but include limitations or restricions until payment is made. Shareware usually carries a lower cost than retail packaged versions because of cost saving in packaging and support. Often these package will expire (i.e. stop working) after a set number of days, or operate with limited functionality until a registration code is entered.

Both freeware and shareware applications are avail-able on the CD. Give these a try and see what you like.

Other software package are also available for download. Look in the Web Links section of the disk for more tools.

Web Links

Links to major web-sites in over a dozen categories:

- Auctions
- Books
- Directories/Search Engines
- Documents & Records
- Organizations
- Travel
- Software
  & more...

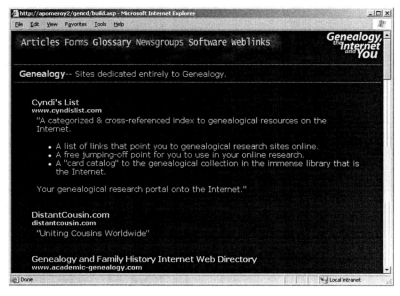

Many of these sites were developed specifically for genealogist. Other sites service the general public and researchers in all fields. The sites are meant to cover the general scope of needs a genealogist might encounter in research. You will find links from supporting technologies to planning family-history excursions. Look up historical records and archives and find local clubs or societies to help you with location specific research.

> *Final Note:* *The collected sites on this CD are guides and starting points. Many are leaders in genealogy research. These sites and tools will help you plan and execute your research. Read and learn new skills and enjoy exploring new content.*